Bizarre Florida: Chronicles of Florida Man

James Christopher

ISBN: 9798321119389

Note to Readers:

Welcome aboard a thrilling voyage through the untamed and perplexing realm of "Florida Man" chronicles. Within these pages lie stories sparked by genuine headlines, plucked from the vast collection of peculiar incidents that seemingly grace only the Sunshine State. While anchored in truth, these tales have been lightly adorned with comedic flair, aiming to encapsulate the essence of the "Florida Man"—an emblem of all that is bizarre, unexpected, and laughably peculiar in Florida's daily happenings. Embark on this journey with an open heart and a keen sense of humor, and remember, the line between truth and fiction blurs most intriguingly in the beloved state of Florida. Enjoy the ride through this unique landscape, where reality often surpasses even the wildest flights of fancy.

Table of Contents

7. Naked Florida Man Steals Pickup Truck from Dealership, Leads Authorities on Pursuit: A Daring Escape That Left Little to the Imagination.

8. The EpiPen Defense: An Allergy to Drunks – A Florida Woman's Unique Method to Cure Her Sister's Inebriation.

9. Space Force Intruder: Warning of an Intergalactic War – A Man's Quest to Inform the Space Force of an Otherworldly Battle.

10. Witchcraft Scam: The $100K Deception – A Florida Woman's Lucrative Promise of Magical Services.

End of Book Bonus Gallery Included

1. Unclaimed Troubles: The Case of the Cocaine-Wrapped Rascal – An odd claim with nowhere to hide.

In Clearwater, Florida, a place where things can get a bit wild after dark, Patrick Florence, a 34-year-old local, found himself in a situation that sounds like something straight out of a comedy sketch. It all started when he was just riding shotgun in a car, cruising through the night. The car, perhaps trying to stay incognito, forgot a crucial detail – its lights were off. That's a no-go, especially when the local deputies are around, ever vigilant in their nocturnal patrol.

The cops pulled them over, not just for the missing lights but because the driver seemed to have had a bit too much fun earlier in the evening and was driving under the influence.

Oh, and they found some marijuana too. But let's be real, the story takes a turn for the bizarre with Patrick, not the driver.

When the deputies decided to take a closer look inside the car, they found a gun under Patrick's seat. That's when things got really interesting. As they patted him down, they discovered something quite unusual – Patrick was sporting some extra... accessories. Wrapped around his private parts were baggies of meth and cocaine. Yes, you read that right. It's not every day you hear about someone using their nether regions as a storage unit for illegal substances.

But here's the kicker: Patrick insisted those drugs weren't his. That's right, despite the drugs being quite literally attached to him, he claimed they belonged to someone else.

The deputies must have had a hard time keeping a straight face when writing up that report. "The package wrapped around his penis was not his," they quoted him saying. Now, that's a line you don't forget easily.

Charged with possession of cocaine, meth, ammunition, and a firearm, Patrick now faced more than just a slap on the wrist. Turns out, this wasn't his first rodeo with the law; he'd been arrested over 20 times for drug-related offenses. You'd think he'd come up with more creative excuses by now.

As for the driver, they didn't get off scot-free either, what with the DUI and marijuana possession charges. But let's be honest, they're just a footnote in the saga of Patrick and his incredible claim of innocence.

So, what have we learned from this tale?

If you're going to carry illegal drugs around, maybe don't wrap them around your private parts. And definitely don't claim they're not yours if you do. It's a story that's bizarre, a bit outlandish, and one that could only happen in Florida.

FLORD
FORY
SERT1 LO
SSHIY
SHEDG
MASK
CHOICE
MATTERS

2. Florida Man Banned from Airline for Wearing Thong as Mask, Compares Himself to Rosa Parks – A Bizarre Protest That Became a National Story.

In the sunny, sometimes topsy-turvy world of Florida, Adam Jenne decided to take fashion to new heights—or should we say, face heights? On a seemingly routine flight from Fort Lauderdale to Washington D.C., Adam turned heads, not with a flashy new hat or a statement T-shirt (though his "Let's go Brandon" attire did catch some eyes), but with a bold choice in facial attire: a skimpy red g-string, artfully placed over his head and face as his version of a mask.

Now, Adam wasn't new to the game of unconventional face coverings. He'd pulled this stunt more than a dozen times, sailing through the skies with his unique mask without much fuss.

Each flight was a roll of the dice, met with reactions ranging from "wild appreciation" to the less enthusiastic "confrontational." But Adam, a connoisseur of reactions, found the variety quite exhilarating.

However, this particular flight was destined for a different script. The TSA and airport security didn't share the previous crews' appreciation or confrontation. Instead, they chose action, and Adam found himself escorted off the plane faster than you could say "fashion police."

But Adam, ever the optimist and philosopher, drew parallels between his plight and that of Rosa Parks, the "first lady of civil rights." He saw his thong-clad protest not just as a statement on airline mask policies but as a stand against "injustice" and "nonsense."

According to Adam, Covid-19 had no clue if humans were cruising at altitude, making the whole mask mandate a theater of the absurd.

And in a twist straight out of a feel-good movie, a dozen fellow passengers, moved by Adam's cause—or perhaps just baffled by the spectacle—decided to make their exit in solidarity. "Did he just get kicked off for wearing a mask? I'm out of here," one declared, leading a mini-exodus in support of Adam's fashion-forward protest.

Adam's parting words were a mix of gratitude for his impromptu followers and a reaffirmation of his beliefs. He saw the whole ordeal as a stand against the nonsensical, a fight for the right to bring absurdity to light with absurdity itself.

With a refunded ticket in his pocket and a spirit undeterred, Adam planned to take his thong-mask crusade to the skies once more, ready to face whatever came next with a cheeky smile hidden beneath his unconventional mask.

In the world of Florida Man tales, Adam Jenne's story stands out as a quirky testament to the lengths some will go to make a statement, no matter how unconventional the method or the attire.

3. Bubble Runner's Oceanic Misadventure – A Daring Attempt to Traverse the Ocean in a Homemade Vessel.

In the sandy stretches of Flagler County, Florida, beachgoers were in for a peculiar sight that redefined the phrase "rolling into the weekend." Reza Baluchi, an adventurer with a dream bigger than his vessel, washed ashore inside what can only be described as a hybrid bubble-running wheel device, akin to a barrel with ambitions of maritime glory.

Baluchi, aiming to turn the Atlantic into his personal treadmill, had set off from St. Augustine with sights set on New York or perhaps even Bermuda. The vessel, a large barrel-type contraption with flotation buoys for shoes, was his steed in this ambitious quest.

The Flagler County Sheriff's Office, ever vigilant on social media, shared snapshots of Baluchi's curious craft, which had beachgoers scratching their heads and reaching for their phones. It wasn't long before the U.S. Coast Guard was called in to ensure that Baluchi and his bubble were up to code for the journey ahead.

Unfortunately, instead of heading north, Baluchi found himself making an unexpected pit stop 30 miles south, courtesy of what he described as "complications."

Fox 35 Orlando caught up with the aspiring bubble runner, who shared his philanthropic vision behind the stunt.

 Baluchi wasn't just chasing horizons; he was running for a cause.

From raising money for the homeless to supporting public services like the coast guard and the fire department, his mission was as multifaceted as his mode of transportation was unconventional. "Chase your dreams," he urged, a living testament to the adage that if you want something done right, you might as well do it in a giant bubble.

However, not all was smooth sailing for Baluchi. The Sun-Sentinel reported a hiccup in his plans when he discovered some of his vital safety and navigation gear missing, stolen by spirits not as adventurous as his own. But like any good story, this one too had a silver lining: the equipment was recovered, and Baluchi's resolve only strengthened. With an eye on the weather and his heart set on the horizon, he plans to resume his bubble-bound odyssey.

Baluchi's journey isn't a first-time endeavor. His YouTube channel and website reveal a history of bubble voyages, including a planned circuit that would make even seasoned sailors raise an eyebrow: from Miami up the coast and into the Bermuda Triangle, then onto Puerto Rico, Haiti, Cuba, and Key West, all while subsisting on a diet that would make a castaway cringe.

So, if you ever find yourself doubting the feasibility of your dreams, remember Reza Baluchi and his bubble. In a world that often tells us to keep our feet firmly on the ground, he reminds us that sometimes, rolling through the waves in a giant bubble barrel is just the perspective shift we need.

4. The Smuggler's Prosthetic: A Jailhouse Surprise – An Innovative but Failed Attempt at Drug Smuggling.

In the sunny sprawl of Pinellas County, where the unusual becomes the norm, Keith Adams, 37, found himself in a particularly tight spot—or tight leg, to be more precise. Adams, a resident of Largo, decided to take "walking on the wild side" to a new level by allegedly using his prosthetic leg as a mobile pharmacy.

The saga begins on a typical Florida Saturday night, when Adams was stopped by local law enforcement. It wasn't long before they discovered he was allegedly carrying a pipe with a penchant for cocaine. But Keith's adventures in unconventional storage were only getting started.

Before being whisked away to the county's least desirable overnight accommodation, officers, perhaps inspired by a hunch or a stroke of procedural diligence, inquired about the contents of Keith's prosthetic leg. "Anything to declare?" they might as well have asked, as if the leg were luggage and the jail a border crossing. Keith, maintaining his poker face, assured them his leg was merely a leg and nothing more.

However, like the most unexpected twist in a Florida Man tale, officers at the jail discovered Keith's leg was harboring secrets: a gram of fentanyl and some Xanax pills. It appears the leg wasn't just supporting Keith; it was also supporting a small but significant drug operation.

The Smoking Gun, that bastion of bizarre news, reported that Keith faced additional charges for his innovative but ill-advised smuggling attempt. The charges stacked up like a deck of cards against him, turning a bad night into a significantly worse one.

Officers had warned Keith, giving him the opportunity to come clean about his hidden stash before entering the jail. However, Keith opted for silence, a choice that would soon come back to haunt him when the concealed cargo was discovered.

Keith's story serves as a cautionary tale, reminding us that while necessity might be the mother of invention, not all inventions are wise—especially when they involve turning a prosthetic limb into a secret compartment.

As for Keith, one can only hope this misadventure leads to a reconsideration of hiding spots in the future.

5. Alligator Wrestling: A Trash Can Confrontation – A man's Backyard Battle with an Unexpected Visitor.

In the land of endless sunshine and the occasional alligator wandering into suburbia, Mount Dora, Florida, became the backdrop for an episode that could only be dubbed "Florida Man Meets Gator." The star of our show, 26-year-old Eugene Bozzi, not your average knight in shining armor but rather a dad and a U.S. Army veteran armed with nothing but a recycling bin and a daring plan.

The adventure began when Eugene's kids spotted what they thought was a baby alligator near their home. However, upon inspection, Eugene realized this was no tiny reptile but a full-grown gator. With the neighborhood kids playing outside, Eugene knew he had to act.

His protective instincts kicked in, not with a sword and shield, but with the modern-day equivalent: a trash can.

Approaching the alligator with the open bin, Eugene became a real-life example of "improvise, adapt, overcome." The gator, perhaps misunderstanding the situation as a strange human attempt at communication, started backing away. Eugene, narrating his own wildlife documentary, awaited the perfect moment to trap the unexpected visitor. "Let me know when the head goes inside," he instructed, as if the alligator would comply on cue.

With a swift movement, the lid closed, and the gator was caught. The scene must have looked like a magician's trick gone awry, but there it was: an alligator in a trash can.

The crowd of about 40 onlookers erupted into cheers, their applause echoing through the neighborhood. A mother even thanked Eugene profusely, likely relieved that her afternoon wouldn't be spent explaining the finer points of alligator safety to her children.

Eugene's feat didn't just make him a local hero; it catapulted him to internet fame as the video of his daring capture went viral. Viewers around the globe were simultaneously amused and relieved that they weren't the ones having to deal with an alligator in their front yard.

After the excitement settled, Eugene wheeled his captive down to a nearby lake, releasing the alligator back into the wild. The gator, probably as confused as it was relieved, wasted no time disappearing into the water, likely pondering its strange encounter with human ingenuity.

So, what's the takeaway from our tale? In Florida, even trash day can turn into an impromptu wildlife rescue mission. Eugene Bozzi, armed with only a bin and a whole lot of courage, reminded us all that sometimes, the best way to solve a problem is with a bit of creativity, bravery, and a willingness to jump into action. And maybe, just maybe, let the professionals handle the alligators next time.

MECOMING
Queen!

6. The Homecoming Election Hack: A Family Affair – A Mother and Daughter's Digital Manipulation for a Crown.

In the tranquil town of Pensacola, where high school homecomings are as revered as Thanksgiving parades, Emily Rose Grover and her mother, Laura Rose Carroll, spun a web of digital intrigue worthy of a Netflix drama. Emily, a teen on the cusp of adulthood, and her mother, an assistant principal with tech savvy, allegedly embarked on a quest not for gold, but for a crown: the illustrious title of Homecoming Queen at Tate High School.

This tale began in the autumnal glow of October when ambitions soared higher than Florida's palm trees.

Laura, wielding her access to the school district's internal system like a modern-day Merlin, cast not spells, but votes—hundreds of them, all in a bid to secure her daughter's victory. But as the leaves turned and fell, so too did the facade of this electoral escapade.

By November, whispers of unauthorized access and a flurry of votes from a singular IP address set the school district abuzz. Investigators, donning their digital detective hats, traced the cyber breadcrumbs back to devices nestled within the Carroll household. The revelation? A total of 246 votes for the homecoming court emanated from there, casting a shadow over the election's integrity.

Students at Tate High, perhaps emboldened by the investigative spirit, shared tales of Emily boasting about her mother's digital dexterity.

It was revealed that since August 2019, Laura's account had been a veritable key to the kingdom, accessing hundreds of high school records, with a significant chunk belonging to Tate students.

Despite Laura's adherence to password protocols and her up-to-date training on the 'Staff Responsible Use of Guidelines for Technology,' her digital dalliances led to a suspension from her role at Bellview Elementary School. As for Emily, the crown she sought to win through digital manipulation resulted in her expulsion from Tate High School.

Charged with an ensemble of felonies related to computer misuse and identity theft, mother and daughter now face the music, potentially a 16-year symphony behind bars.

Eventually, court records show Carroll pleaded no contest Sept. 8, 2022 to one count of use of a two-way communication device to facilitate a felony, according to the Escambia County Clerk of Court. Adjudication was withheld, and Carroll was sentenced to 18 months of probation and ordered to pay court costs totaling $518.

7. Naked Florida Man Steals Pickup Truck from Dealership, Leads Authorities on Pursuit: A Daring Escape That Left Little to the Imagination.

In Melbourne, Florida, a tale unfolds that's bound to make headlines and raise eyebrows—possibly even both at the same time. Meet Richard Blose, a 40-year-old man whose penchant for automotive theft is only matched by his aversion to clothing. Our story begins in the early hours at Fiat of Melbourne, where an unsuspecting employee encounters Richard in a paint booth. However, Richard isn't there for a touch-up job; instead, he's in his birthday suit, perhaps mistaking the dealership for a very exclusive spa.

Without a stitch on, Richard makes his grand exit, not on foot, but in a 2021 Ram truck, freshly liberated from the dealership.

Surveillance footage reveals that Richard's arrival at the dealership was somewhat of a prelude, as he was first spotted in only his underwear, engaging in an eclectic mix of vehicle exploration and rooftop meditation.

The plot thickens as Richard, now clothed in nothing but the wind, takes the stolen Ram on a joyride down Interstate 95. His driving is erratic, marked by an intimate acquaintance with a guardrail, suggesting perhaps he's less accustomed to the power of a Ram than he is to the freedom of nudity.

The Melbourne Police, in a chase as riveting as it is bizarre, finally apprehend Richard after a pursuit that likely had onlookers questioning their morning coffee. Taken into custody, Richard faces a slew of charges, his bond denied as if to say, "No shirt, no shoes, no service—or freedom, for that matter."

In a twist that could only happen in Florida, neighbors reveal that Richard's escapade is not his first foray into public disrobing, hinting at a habitual streak that has them concerned for the community's fabric (both moral and textile).

As for Richard's defense? A mysterious figure in a red shirt, apparently the mastermind behind the vehicular heist. One can't help but wonder if this elusive character was the same genius advising Richard on his wardrobe choices.

Richard's adventures land him back in the Brevard County Jail, a place he's become all too familiar with. Meanwhile, the residents of Longbow Road and the wider Melbourne community are left to ponder the age-old question: What's more alarming, the theft or the method of the thief's attire?

In the end, this Floridian escapade serves as a reminder that truth is often stranger than fiction, especially when it comes to the exploits of the infamous "Florida Man."

EPPEN

8. The EpiPen Defense: An Allergy to Drunks – A Florida Woman's Unique Method to Cure Her Sister's Inebriation.

In Naples, Florida, where the sun sets over the Gulf and the palm trees sway, a peculiar tale of sisterly discord unfolded. Joanna Zielinski, 62, and her sister found themselves embroiled in an incident that's sure to be recounted at family gatherings for years to come, perhaps with a mix of horror and disbelief.

The evening began innocuously enough, with the two sisters sharing drinks and presumably, laughter. But as the night wore on, one sister's eyelids grew heavy with sleep, a stark contrast to Joanna, whose party was just getting started.

What transpired next could only originate from the most imaginative corners of a Florida Man (or Woman) headline: Joanna, perhaps inspired by a bizarre cocktail of concern and alcohol-induced logic, decided to address her sister's inebriation in the most unconventional way possible. Armed with an EpiPen, she declared herself "allergic to drunks" and proceeded to "treat" her sister's condition by administering multiple jabs with the life-saving device, including a notable one to the left thigh that left its mark.

When the authorities arrived, prompted by a mysterious 911 call hang-up, they were greeted by this bizarre scene. Joanna's explanation to the bewildered officers was as straightforward as it was perplexing: why not cure drunkenness with an EpiPen if one is allergic?

Despite her innovative approach to sobriety, the police were unamused. It turns out, the EpiPen, while indeed prescribed to Joanna, wasn't quite the miracle cure for alcohol she hoped it to be. In fact, her sister wasn't injected with any medication at all, owing to a flawed technique in wielding the device.

The revelation that Joanna's sister harbored no allergies did little to clarify the situation. What did become clear, however, was a history of violence that led to Joanna's arrest on a charge of battery - domestic violence.

As Joanna was escorted away, one can only imagine the thoughts running through her head.

Was it regret? Confusion? Or perhaps the lingering question of why, if at all, EpiPens can't cure drunkenness. Meanwhile, Naples added another story to its collection, a tale that serves as a reminder that Florida never ceases to surprise, and that perhaps some allergies are best left untreated.

SPACE FORCE BASE
STOP
FLORIDUH
LO

9. Space Force Intruder: Warning of an Intergalactic War – A Man's Quest to Inform the Space Force of an Otherworldly Battle.

In an episode that blurs the line between reality and the plot of a sci-fi blockbuster, a man in Florida embarked on a mission so bizarre it could only fit into the annals of "Florida Man" lore. Corey Allan Johnson, aged 29 and hailing from Ocala, found himself in the grip of presidential directives—albeit, ones communicated telepathically. The message was urgent: warn the Space Force's Guardians about an imminent war not of this world, a conflict raging between U.S. aliens and Chinese dragons.

Johnson's chosen steed for his quest was a stolen Ford F-150, spirited away three days before he made his daring approach to the gates of Patrick Space Force Base in Brevard County. Upon his arrest by local deputies, Johnson shared his tale of cosmic diplomacy and interstellar warfare, a narrative prompted by none other than the President's voice in his head.

The stolen truck, which Johnson confessed to taking without knowledge of its owner, was intended to carry him onto the base to deliver his critical message. Yet, despite his convictions, he was halted before he could breach the perimeter, arrested for grand theft auto. His mission to alert the guardians of the galaxy—earthbound though they might be—was left uncompleted.

Patrick Space Force Base, the backdrop of this intergalactic bulletin, is itself embroiled not in celestial combat but in the earthly tasks of establishing its presence and capabilities. A relative newcomer among military branches, its focus lies in satellite launches, operations, and assuming responsibilities from other military sectors. Whether its jurisdiction covers the defense against extraterrestrial dragons remains a matter for debate.

Speculation abounds on how the U.S. military, including the Space Force, would respond to such a fantastical threat. Imaginations run wild with visions of a joint task force, combining the expertise and firepower of all military branches to confront an Alien-Dragon war.

The Space Force, with its cadre of space-savvy computer experts, would likely play a crucial role in logistics, intelligence, and cyber operations, ensuring that the skies—both earthly and beyond—remain secure.

This tale of "Florida Man" versus the forces of the universe adds yet another chapter to the state's legacy of strange but true stories, leaving us to ponder the thin line between the mundane and the magical, the terrestrial and the celestial.

100K MAGICAL
SERVICES

10. Witchcraft Scam: The $100K Deception – A Florida Woman's Lucrative Promise of Magical Services.

In sunny Naples, Florida, a place where the breeze carries whispers of mystique and magic, Rosalia, a crafty enchantress (or so she claimed), wove a spell not of love or fortune but of deception, coaxing $100,000 from the pockets of those desperate for a touch of the supernatural in their love lives.

Rosalia, casting herself as a purveyor of "witchcraft services," promised to mend broken hearts and heal rifts in relationships through her profound spiritual insights and rituals. From January to March, her ads sang siren songs across free Hispanic newspapers, radio waves, and even fluttered like mystical leaves in laundromats and stores across the Golden Gate and East Naples areas.

"Trouble with your beloved? Fear not, for Rosalia can ease your woes," her ads seemed to declare.

Alas, the promise of divine intervention was but a mirage. At least ten lovelorn souls, seduced by the prospect of curing their romantic ailments, handed over their hard-earned cash to Rosalia. Four of these hopeful romantics parted with significant sums, money that Rosalia claimed required cleansing but instead seemed to vanish into thin air.

One particularly poignant tale involved a man entranced by Rosalia's assurances that she could see a "dark" shadow over his life. With a heart heavy with hope, he entrusted her with $29,500, a fortune that Rosalia promised to bless and multiply.

Yet, the only darkness lay in her intentions, for she claimed this money too was tainted and needed purification at her temple—a temple that must have been built on foundations of deceit, for once the money was in her hands, Rosalia disappeared like a ghost in the night, leaving behind nothing but silence and unanswered messages.

The victims, bewitched by promises of spiritual salvation for their love lives, found themselves instead ensnared in a web of lies. It's a tale as old as time, a reminder that when it comes to matters of the heart, there are no quick fixes, no matter how enchanting the offer may seem. Rosalia's magic proved to be nothing more than smoke and mirrors, a costly illusion that left her patrons not with mended hearts but lighter wallets.

In the end, this Florida "witch" brewed a potion too potent for her own good, as the law caught up with her sleight of hand, leaving us to ponder the age-old adage: if something seems too magical to be true, it probably is.

Please Enjoy a Bonus Gallery of an Eventual Part 2: Florida Man! Can you Guess the Headlines?

LIFETIME BAN
WORLD'S BEST DAD
LIFETIME

#####!!!##Q
FLORIDA CLUB
NO CATS ALLOWED
FLORIDA
MAIN
NO PETS

FLORIDA
LIVE GRENADE

1.339

TIME TRAVEL
PLAZA
WELCOME TO
TIME TRAVEL